THERE'S AN ALCOHOLIC IN THE FAMILY ...

AND IT'S ME!

Support & Insights
for your
First 30 days in Recovery

Jason S. Whitehead

Kindle Publishing
Create Space
Copyright 2016 by Jason S. Whitehead
All rights reserved. Published 2016
Printed in the United States of America

No part of this publication may be reproduced, stored in a retrieval system, or transmitted in any form or by any means—electronic, mechanical, photocopying, recording, scanning, or otherwise—without the express written permission of the author. Failure to comply with these terms may expose you to legal action and damages for copyright infringement.

Library of Congress Cataloging info upon request
ISBN – 10: 1540739228
ISBN – 13: 978-1540739223

ABOUT THE AUTHOR

That's me: 41, single, a football fanatic, and hiding behind sunglasses.

As alcoholics we are good at hiding: our bottles, mistakes, heartaches, fears, and disease. AA tells us we need to hide behind a wall of anonymity. WHY? The answer is simple and unjust: society doesn't recognize we have a disease and that the cure is treatment—long-term, lifelong treatment. Instead we are misunderstood, labeled, judged, incarcerated, and outcast.

We feel doomed to self-destruction, many times without the support of loved ones or friends. It's certainly not a road any of us would choose. We don't get up in the morning and determine: "Today would be a great day to ruin my life, relationships, security, and career."

Our only hope is support from those who understand, because they have walked this lonely, frightening, and oft discouraging road. I'm breaking anonymity, and speaking out about the horrors of our disease for two reasons.

First, I want to encourage you, my fellow traveller, because there is hope; we can and do recover.

Together let's find a way to join hands through these pages over the next thirty days and walk this thing out one day at a time.

Secondly, I'm hopeful the day will come when we can be open and honest about our disease and receive the understanding and medical attention we need and deserve. I've met so many amazing men and women who suffer from alcoholism. We aren't a partying group; we are hurting. We need healing. We are, however, intelligent, creative, caring, loving, and tenderhearted men and women, husbands and wives, children and parents, grandparents, aunts and uncles; we are leaders and coworkers. We are of great value to our families and communities.

Your first thirty days are just the beginning of a lifetime commitment; but they will be your hardest days. So reach deep. Make my commitment below, your commitment, and together let's take these first critical steps in this thing called recovery.

MY COMMITMENT

"I'm Jason Whitehead, and I am an alcoholic,

but with the help of my friends, my family,

and my God,

NO MATTER WHAT,

I WILL NOT DRINK!"

DEDICATION

This book is dedicated . . .

To my dad, Stan, who has picked me up more times than any dad should,

To my step-mom, Maria, who has welcomed me into her heart,

To my sister Tamie, who has never judged me or stopped loving me in spite of myself,

To Hank and Carol Akin who have loved me unconditionally, always believed in me, and walked this thing out with me,

A special thanks to Carol who has pulled this book out of me and is largely responsible for its being,

To Nyla, my pug, who has nurtured my soul with her own special brand of love and healing, and

To all those who have lent a word of encouragement, a listening ear, friendship, professional advice, or a helping hand on my journey.

IN LOVING MEMORY
of my beloved mother

Kathryn (Kathy) Fisher Whitehead
(1948 – 1987)

THERE'S AN ALCOHOLIC
IN THE FAMILY . . .*AND IT'S ME!*

TABLE OF CONTENTS

Introduction 8

The Common Bond of Suffering 13

Day Two 20

A Silent Cry for Help 28

Something to Live For 33

The Caregiver 39

Honesty: The True Indicator of Change 45

Less Than 53

What a Difference a Day Makes 57

Temptation Alley 63

Paradise Lost 69

Rainy Days 74

The People Under the Stairs 78

Risk, Reward, & Reality 83

Self-Image 90

What Are They Thinking? 95

The Angry Face of Friendship 101

Mechanical Failure 104

Maybe We Took This Too Far 108

The Chronic Relapser 114

A Room Without Walls 118

Alone with a Monster 124

Will You Be There? 132

Down With the Ship 139

Life without a Crutch 142

Catch Me If You Can 148

Cravings 152

The Devil Inside 159

Have I Arrived 164

Be Somebody! 168

Baby Steps 172

Epilogue 177

THERE'S AN ALCOHOLIC
IN THE FAMILY . . . *AND IT'S ME!*

INTRODUCTION

*"You cannot run away from weakness; you must some
time fight or perish; and if that be so,
why not now, and where you stand."*
Robert Lewis Stevenson (1850-1894) Scotland

How are you today? Feeling up? Feeling down?

Does it even matter? For our purposes, it doesn't. You

are totally beyond feeling today; damaged from life and

all it has to offer. You have moved beyond all feeling to

a state of complete numbness.

If you've picked up this book, you are no doubt

at the point you just wish you could get away from

yourself, possibly forever. It's the feeling you'd like to

rise up, leaving this numb version of yourself, and be

resurrected to who you used to be, or to who you know

you really should be. Isn't that why we take things as far as we do? Aren't we just trying to get out of ourselves?

Well, I'm here to tell you, you've been chasing the wrong solutions in the wrong ways. Well, duh! You know this already. But if you hear nothing else I've written in these pages, just know things can and will change.

I know you may want to throw this book at me, because you've no room left in your mind for even one positive thought about sobriety. But hold on. You'll soon figure out this is not your typical inspirational book. I tell it like it is with all the good, the bad, and the ugly—no sugar coating. Furthermore, I mean what I say, because it is born from painful experience and not clinical theories. So give a listen.

We are going to walk through the mire together for the next thirty days, picking up one foot at a time until we find solid ground so we can take a step 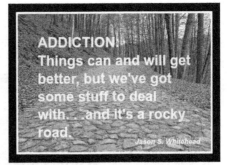 forward. Things WILL get better, but we've got some stuff to deal with and it's a rocky road.

So give me thirty days, test it, and walk it out with me. My thirty-day promise to you is this: stay sober and see if: 1) people start to matriculate slowly back into your life, and 2) your attitudes and emotions significantly change. Your friends and family have been programmed to expect the worst in you to show up. They have all but forgotten the *good* you. Maybe you've all but forgotten him, too. But if you are still reading, then I'm betting you know he is still there somewhere deep inside. So let's bring him back to life. When others experience the *good* you again, they will be delighted. So will you.

Read a chapter in this little book every day. Unfortunately, I know you will likely relate to the musings. Let me put my arm around your shoulder as you take these few first steps in the right direction.

This isn't your typical recovery book. I'm coming at this recovery thing a different way. I simply want to walk through the first painful days with you right where you are. At least in the beginning, I think there is value in getting real; so let's face the filth we have created in an open and honest way. And then maybe, just maybe, after some of the anger, frustration, and resentment begin to dissipate, you can let a little positive energy seep back into your life. Maybe you will find the strength to shed the pain that has engulfed you like a cloak for a new set of active wear that will let you breathe and effectively run the race of life.

"The best way out is always through."
-Robert Frost (1874-1963) USA

THE COMMON BOND OF SUFFERING

When I was growing up, it seemed for one reason or another, people always wanted to share their secrets and difficult emotions with me. I found myself listening for hours, sometimes about things I wished I'd never heard. Rather than walking away excited by the dirt I now possessed, I felt confused and often gazed off into the horizon wondering, "Why me?" I was a magnet for hurt people. Maybe it was because I was a good listener or trustworthy, but I'm sure it more likely had something to do with the fact I was hurting too. I wanted to be able to heal those people. I searched in vain for the exact right thing to say to make them feel better. As I listened, I wished I had the one perfect piece of advice to just fix it all.

No doubt my advice was never really all that great, and rarely did it help anyone. So I kept bouncing along through life, listening to people's problems, and creating a host of my own. I even studied psychology in college, hoping I would be able to make a career out of my knack for empathy. All the while I was really trying to figure out how to cure myself. As sad as it is true, I didn't accomplish either. The harder I tried to understand myself, the worse things got. I eventually landed in a bottle, which landed me in a couple of different treatment centers for alcoholism.

The last organization offered me the opportunity to become a peer counselor; I was given a caseload of men to oversee and the daily assignment of teaching classes. Finally, I had an outlet to share my thoughts on something I was truly an expert in: alcohol addiction. Clients were sharing with me their horrific tales and experiences of substance abuse that I truly understood, and many times had experienced myself. It was like a dream come true. I was even actually pretty good at teaching the classes. The men I mentored really seemed to like and relate to the things I had to say. Over time, I'd watch them graduate from the program, one after the other, many of them citing me as a major contributor to their sobriety. I had found my calling. A life of pain and emotional turmoil had finally become useful for something other than fuel for my drinking binges.

All the praise and satisfaction of my seemingly good work was short-lived; one by one more than half of my protégés found their way back through the doors of the program. It should come as no surprise I stumbled back through those very same doors just a couple of years later.

No longer do I expect to be able to heal anyone or to solve his or her problems in and of my own power. I can't will you (or even myself) into sobriety. There is no magic formula to make all your troubles go away. It's safe to say I can't even do those things for myself.

After all the years of listening, sympathizing, and advising people on their various issues, I realized something Dr. Foster Kennedy, neurologist, put perfectly in the book *Alcoholics Anonymous*: "This organization of Alcoholics Anonymous calls on two of the greatest reserves of power known to man, religion and that instinct for association with one's fellows--the 'herd instinct.'" [1]

I didn't write this book with any fantasy it had healing powers; nor do I think it will get you (or anyone else) sober on its own merit. I wrote it so someone who feels as awkward and alone with their thoughts and feelings as I did, would know they are not alone. I hope you will gain some small comfort in knowing there is someone who understands and relates to everything you are going through.

"Judge no man before you have walked two moons in his moccasins"
- Native American Proverb

---

[1] Dr. Foster Kennedy, *Alcoholics Anonymous*, Appendix III, The Medical View on A.A. (Alcoholics Anonymous World Services, Inc. 1939) 569.

My singular hope, as you read through this book, is that you may find a story, an idea, or maybe a whole chapter you can really

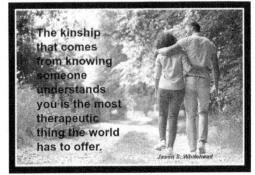

sink your teeth into and say, "I know exactly how that feels." The kinship that comes from knowing someone understands you is the most therapeutic thing the world has to offer. The rest is up to you and your Higher Power.

So if this is your first day and you cannot sit up, keep food on your stomach, think a sane thought, or even muster up enough hope to dream of a life of sobriety, just know you aren't the only one. I've been there; thousands of others have walked this same horrific and lonely road. Many of us have made it; you can, too. Take a deep breath. Try to keep some food on your stomach. Get as much rest as you can. Put off trying to figure out the whys and muddling through the regrets of your actions until you are sober. They will still be there then, and you can make more sense of it all with some help and time under your belt. So maybe you can just set all that aside for now. Most importantly, don't try to carry the weight of all the problems of the rest of your life on your shoulders today. You've got enough to deal with just trying to get through the day. You can do this just for today.

So walk with me, and let's face the fact we are indeed the alcoholics in our families and we need help. Hold fast for today!

"Agenda for today: breathe out, breathe in,
breathe out."
-Buddha

DAY TWO

So are you sick again, watching daytime television, bad movies, and doing anything you can to avoid people, your own thoughts, and the impending doom of the days ahead? Sometimes it's easier to watch a mindless zombie movie than it is to consider your own carnivorous and insatiable methods that erode the foundations of the people around you. Can you relate?

During one of these hung-over days of my life, I watched a movie about a kid who set out to procure medicine for his baby brother because his mom told him he could not return without it. Without the money to make the purchase, he went so far as to steal a gun from his granddad's bathroom. In my own way, I could relate. It wasn't that I knew anything about a baby brother dying for lack of medicine, or even the inevitable armed robbery that was about to take place. What I did understand was the hurricane dark cloud feeling that comes over you when there are no more options at your disposal. It feels like you are faced with an impossible dilemma. Just like the kid in the movie who could not see any other possibilities, your course of action narrows and so does your perspective. In this time you struggle to understand yourself and your own thinking, much less the world around you. Some call it tunnel vision. I call it the brink of insanity.

You just need that one thing: a job, rent, or probably just a drink. It's irrelevant what it is you think you need, because the feeling is all the same. It's desperation. And I don't mean desperation like your car has a flat or that it's just started raining and you're without an umbrella. I'm talking about a desperation all its own. It's a hopelessness, contrived from the depths of your own soul, driving you to the point where there is almost nothing you wouldn't do to obtain whatever it is you feel is that one right thing: the one thing you have convinced yourself will make it all better.

This was the type of desperation the boy in the movie was facing. The irony to the film was he was shot and killed during his attempted robbery. Maybe that's why my own desperation never sent me to rob a store or murder someone. It's the harsh reality that keeps most of us from completely flying off the deep end. We maintain a semblance of reasoning, despite our own seemingly innate desire to abandon it all.

I realize God is practically a curse word for some of you, but God surely does not want this for us. Surely we were created for more. Where does this propensity for self-destruction come from? How did we get to this point of desperation? Is it of the devil?

The fact is it's not even self-destruction really; it's abandonment—abandonment of self. How can I get off this vessel of loathing anyway? My ship set sail some 41 years ago and I never asked to board. My ticket was just punched; and next thing I knew, I was sitting poolside on the Jason Whitehead cruise liner. One problem: It was not luxurious. The activity calendar looked great on the brochure, but the whole thing was a flop. Did I plot my course on the wrong ship of life? Did I even have a choice?

Can you relate yet?

So let's talk about the positive for a moment. YES, there is a positive side. All that crap about destruction and despair and abandonment is all a self-imposed lie. Yep, it's a lie. If you're ready to stop reading now, give me a chance to explain. I know, I know, I sound like some hack life coach who's going to pump sunshine in your face until you want to shoot someone with a happiness gun. Nope, not going to do that. I just need you to consider a few things, that's all.

You can remember being happy, can't you? Maybe it was just once; maybe it was a long time ago. Surely it wasn't always this way. Things could have been worse actually, but there was still a little niggle in your mind telling you it hasn't always been this way. Even when you started drinking too heavily, you were still convinced you could manage it. Even when things started going horribly awry, you just knew in the depths of your soul you could set things right. You likely never really had it all together, but you thought you did, or at least hoped you could find the answer to your growing problem. Truth be known, I don't know that any of us ever holds all the answers. In some way we all at least think we have some answers. In its most basic form, and however small, it is simply a belief in ourselves that keeps most of us going.

Hold on to your seat, but it's kind of what it means to believe in God. It's a knowing without knowing or being certain in the uncertain. Belief is the strongest force I've ever known. It can build someone up and take them to the head of the class. It's a concept that tore at me when my parents would say, "You can be whatever you want to be, Jason." What a bunch of hooey! Or was it? As I began to believe my life was hopeless and over, it became just that. And because I believed the lies, things became even worse; I became exactly what I believed I could, or would, become. Somewhere along the line, I just quit believing I could be anything, let alone anything good.

Chances are you quit believing in yourself somewhere along the line, too. Of course you did. You're just like me. The worse I became, the worse I believed I would become. And so things got even worse. There's now a plaque hanging in my room; it says, "You can become anything you believe you can become." So I work on the voices I let in and choose carefully the tapes I allow to play in my mind.

Maybe you can relate now. The point I'm trying to make is that you must harness the power of belief for good in your life, the same as you did for the bad. Even if you are not an alcoholic or addict and you just wanted to peek into the alcoholic mind, the principle stands.

I'm not going to end with puppy dogs and rainbows today because I know from experience you are not feeling either one. But I said there was something positive and there is. It can act as a remedy to the belief we are doomed. It's an anecdote or a magic elixir of sorts. It's called HOPE. It's hard to see it right now. I barely see it sometimes, but I know it's there. I've seen it before and it exists. Hope is not a fairy tale, a myth, or an urban legend. It's out there for all of us. As they say in the support groups, "Hold on for one more day!"

So know you aren't the only one who has been in a desperate state of mind, and hold on. Hold on for dear life. One thing for sure, circumstances change. It will get better. Don't take my word for it; take your own. You won't believe anyone but yourself, but it's ok to hope someone like me just might be right.

"You cannot prevent the birds of sadness from flying over your head, but you can prevent them from nesting in your hair."
- Chinese Proverb

A SILENT CRY FOR HELP

We've all heard the visceral cry of a child, where the depth of their distress becomes so intense it goes from shrill, earth rattling shrieks to the vaguely audible sound of a dog whistle. They are crying so hard there is in fact no more sound. It's almost like a gasping for air rather than crying. Suffice it to say, I'm sure we've not only heard this, but that we have in fact, also done it ourselves.

Scientifically, I have no idea why this happens. It appears the emotional drain is so intense, the body is unable to produce the otherwise alarming and informative sounds of crying, despite the child's apparent need for attention. In this same way, the alcoholic has been consumed by a pain so great, that despite his/her inward desire to cry out, he is simply unable to do so. It's these barely audible gasps for intervention that both we, as an alcoholic, and your caregivers, friends, and family need to tune our ears to hear. These are our silent cries for help.

So what do these silent cries look and sound like? Well, that's the hard part. They probably come in about as many forms as there are addicts. Regardless of the form, at their heart they are nothing more than a desire to moderate, curb, control, or quit entirely the use of a substance. They will not be sensational confessions for intervention. In fact, most of the time, they will vaguely be sincere on any conscious level.

To illustrate my point, I'm reminded of the classic ruse where someone pretends to cough, but actually mutters something through the distortion of the cough. The prankster is typically attempting to vocalize something they would really like to say but don't have the guts to vocalize. We alcoholics ask for our help in almost the same way.

A short time before we completely fall off the deep end, or perhaps in early recovery when we are struggling, we begin to drop subtle clues we may need some help. We give hints perhaps there are some things we need to change. The truth is we absolutely need help and there are some  things we must change: IMMEDIATELY. We realize we have to act fast without overreacting.

Our passive cries for help have a short lifespan. As the alcoholic, you need to realize you're probably not just having a bad day. You are crying out to yourself just as much as you are to others. So, if help comes your way or is available: TAKE IT!

One thing about addiction that makes its stranglehold on our lives so unbreakable is our seeming inability to ask for, and in many cases even want help. Despite what we know, feel, and see is happening to our lives, we stay stuck in our punctured-hull life raft, hoping we will someday sail off into the sunset of our own personal mastery of the very thing that is killing us. Since no one ever regains control once it's lost, and your chances of going cold turkey with no spiritual, mental, or emotional support are practically nonexistent, then it's probably time to abandon that sinking ship and get on board someone else's boat.

If you only need therapy, then you should at least ask for, then go, and actually participate in therapy. If you have been feeling like it's time to get connected or reconnected at church, then it's high time you do so. If you just want to see what an AA meeting might be like, go to one. If you think you may need all of this and a few more things, stop debating, stop waiting, stop crying silently, and go get help now. Talk sincerely with your loved ones about your needs. They aren't mind readers, so help them understand what help you need and how to walk beside you. Today's decisions will become tomorrow's testimonies.

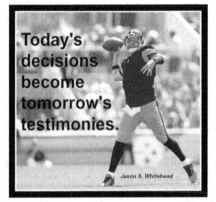

"Just Do It"
- Nike (1988 – Present)

SOMETHING TO LIVE FOR

Too many times in my alcoholism, I came to a place where I thought I would never get back to where I once was; worse yet, I feared I'd never get to where I was supposed to be. Growing up in a private school in the wealthy west end of town cultivated the idea in my adolescent mind I had to be distinguished and rich to be considered a success. The last names in my yearbook read like the who's who of our city. We didn't just have a great college entry rate; we had a 100% college entry rate. Community colleges and technical schools were not part of the equation. It was an automatic expectation we would all get good jobs and live in the suburbs with big homes, large yards, three car garages, and 401K's larger than most people see in twenty years of hard labor.

It soon became obvious my path had veered dramatically from the others. My decision to leave the herd and move south may have been the one that almost cost me my life. My college career looked more like *Animal House* than five years at a place of higher learning. As the drinking became more and more frequent, I attended classes less and less. I soon discovered drinking in the morning was just as fun as drinking at happy hour or after hours. Before I could down my next drink, the dreams of my childhood receded into the ocean of my once optimistic imagination, and the reality of who I had become settled in like a dense fog.

I mucked my way through a few decent jobs I had no business landing in the first place; and one after the other, they receded back into the mire I had created for myself. My will to win was completely gone. The only attainable victory seemed to be scoring another bottle at the liquor store, not getting arrested, or somehow not getting kicked out of whatever rental unit I called home. Somewhere between throwing up in trashcans, the crazy hallucinations, and everyone I ever knew all but disowning me, hope vanished. Even if I could stop drinking, I had gone too far down. I was at the nadir of my own sanity and I wasn't sure I was coming back.

A few years passed and a few more relationships died. I'd climb out of one hole and fall right into the next. I didn't want to live anymore. I wasn't even afraid to die; I just didn't want to kill myself. I was hoping the booze would do that for me. In my mind there was nothing left for which to live.

When you decide it's time to put down the bottle and step out of the wilderness, it is unthinkable that you can ever realize any of the dreams you've drowned out for years. You might even find yourself angrily defiant when someone suggests you can still accomplish all the things you dreamed of doing. You've conditioned yourself for failure for years, maybe even decades. No wonder success at anything, especially plain old sobriety, seems laughable. All the wasted years, lost opportunities, and broken relationships paint a veneer of inadequacy over your mind's eye.

It's not something you're going to be able to overcome with the snap of your fingers, and it will certainly take some time to clean up the wreckage of your past. But, the truth is that all is not lost. There is hope, and even more hope still to come. Things will not only get better, they will indeed get better than you ever dreamed in the first place. You may even find your dreams have changed and the new ones are what you really wanted all along. A lot has changed since you moved under that fog.

Let me be clear on one thing. Some of your broken relationships will return and some may not. Life may return exactly as it was or it may be something completely different. You might even find you have become someone completely different: someone more mature, measured, focused, determined, and responsible.

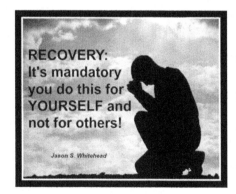

The most important thing you must understand is that you have to do this for yourself. Don't get sober for your wife, kids, boss, parents, or to get your stuff back. Do it for yourself! You see, you absolutely have something for which to live. It is something more near and dear than anything else:

yourself. If you keep this your focus, the rest will follow.

"If your compassion does not include yourself, it is incomplete"
- Buddha (c.563 – c.483)

THE CAREGIVER

The caregiver is a huge thorn in my side. Why do they keep trying so hard to make sure I am happy? What gives them the right to try to control whether or not I am happy? Do they even know why I am upset? Their positive energy makes me so angry. What are they so happy about anyway? I don't want anybody to care. Caring hurts both them and me. Just leave me alone and let me die in peace or pieces, whichever comes first.

So I've got this person in my life who wants nothing more than the best for me. They would buy me another round of tequila on the heels of a weeklong bender, if they thought it would lead to something better. They are so blinded by love, they step on the very last nerve I cling to with my last thread of sanity.

Why do we despise this person's presence? If they left me, I would be alone and more miserable than ever; I really love them and know they love me. "Just leave me alone," I shout, "LEAVE ME ALONE!!" But inside I'm crying, "Don't get too far or stay away too long or I'll run away."

What do our loved ones need to do for us? They need to get away, at least in the short term. We need quiet, not conversation. We need healing, and that takes time. We will soon long for their companionship, but early on we just need to rest our minds and body.

When I began to get sober, the friends in my life bought me a dog, a pug to be specific. She was a gift for me; but, I had no money and no means to care for her. What was I supposed to do with a pug? They were the ones who wanted the pug I surmised, and I conveniently lived with them. From my viewpoint, they got the new dog they wanted for themselves and packaged it as a gift for me. What a joke! That was the truth, but only a half-truth. They really did want me to have the dog. They thought her love would shower over me and erase any feelings of self-loathing and loneliness. Guess what? Almost! She was a special dog, and she did indeed fill my heart and life with love while sweeping away some of those lonely feelings. But, we're a smart bunch, aren't we? We think we see through these things and determine other's intentions aren't pure.

Here's another whammy! It doesn't matter what we think. They wanted good things for me and I didn't see it. Why would anybody do anything that nice for a guy like me? People love us, and we still cannot figure out why. We have people in our lives who want nothing but good things for us, but we never seem to understand it. Why? Stay sober for a few weeks and you will see why.

Its' not going to happen next week. It will take a month, maybe two AT LEAST. But one day, the real you will show up; you know the one. He laughs, hums a tune, kids around, cheers for his team, maps out a great day trip with friends, refinishes a piece of furniture, plants a tree, cleans the garage, plays with the dog, or cooks a spectacular spread for game day. Oh, so maybe this is the guy they love.

Imagine betting on a horse that lost thirty races over the course of three years. Next thing you know, he wins one. Are you going to bet the farm on him the next race? Probably not. How do you think our loved ones feel? You didn't buy this book because you had a bad weekend. So take the love and joy they have to offer today. It may look like they are trying to control your life; e.g., taking your keys and wallet, monitoring your comings and goings, etc. They are just trying to get you to the point where you can take it forward alone. Walk it out with them. You will bite long before they do.

There have been many times I hated the caregivers in my life, too. Just understand, of all people, they are trying their own brand of help, not realizing every good deed is a reminder of our misery and the fact we are undeserving. Even love and joy can hurt.

So, tell them thank you, even if doesn't suit you right now; tell them you need alone time to process your thoughts. Then take a deep breath and thank God someone stills cares for you.

Now get out of bed and do something (even if it is only to take out the trash) so you can look in the mirror this evening and say that just for today, you are deserving of their love and care.

"One of the greatest diseases is to be nobody to anybody"
- Mother Theresa (1910 – 1997)

HONESTY: THE TRUE INDICATOR OF CHANGE

I recently heard a friend say something quite profound: "Being honest with others is easy; being honest with yourself is the true indicator of change."

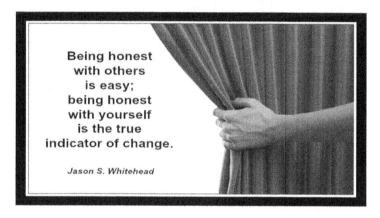

I've known some people, who, at least on the surface, appear to believe their own lies. My dad is one such individual. He can tell a story about an event I was there for as a child. My memory of the event is crystal clear, as if it happened yesterday. Kids don't forget anything, you know. His recollections are of laughter, exaggeration, and intrigue. He's a great storyteller; he's truly one of the best I know. The facts, however, are all his own. I'm certain most of us, including my dad, know exactly when we are exaggerating or lying, and about what, even when it's to ourselves. We lie to ourselves and believe it, because we are seeking a favorable outcome. It's the most basic form of manipulation, even when we are doing it to ourselves.

Did you ever think about how you've manipulated yourself: your thinking and your actions? Isn't that somewhat bizarre? You probably have considered this, if you've been doing it long enough. You know how you sometimes figure your way out of situations, creating plausible lies to cover reality. Then one day, YOU GET CAUGHT! You have no more options and you're pinned down. There's just too much evidence of truth for you to be able to continue in the lies you have fabricated.

Once we face the truth, the next step is self-evaluation. You start asking yourself questions like, "What could I have done differently?" or "At what point did I make the mistake that led to this?" Now get ready for the punch in the mouth. You took one of two options from here:

Option 1) You assessed the situation, examining what went wrong and the damage that would surely ensue, and then planned the next big lie to get what you wanted, or

Option 2) You might be one of those acutely in tune people who realized the real lie is telling yourself you could pull off a lie to begin with. It's not that you couldn't pull it off, but the odds are getting slimmer every time you try.

Let me give you an example and simultaneously show you why what I'm saying is true.

When I lived in White Plains, NY, my drinking was really starting to sprout wings. I had a great job I loved, and I was pretty good at it. It was a territory sales position that sent me flying all over the Southeast with an expense account to ride shotgun. I ate, DRANK, and was merry.

It all finally came to head at a San Francisco trade show I had begged to attend. My boss was there for the first of three days; and a brand new car-salesman type joined us to learn the ropes. After enjoying the first night on the boss, the new guy and I decided to lay low and go to the hotel bar the second night. There was no need to spend money when we had house accounts at the hotel. He and I enjoyed ourselves, but kept it within reason. I sprung for the tab and put it on my room, which in turn would go to the company, as always. No worries; it was just a normal night.

Night three rolled around and we decided the second verse should be the same as the first. Back to the hotel bar, back to the shots, and away we went. Being new and trying to safeguard himself, he decided to skip on the tab and head to the room before things went too far. Being an alcoholic and not caring, I decided to stay and spin the wheel of fortune. I proceeded to have a really big time. I bought drinks for everyone who had a pulse. "Who cares," I thought. "What's the worst that could happen?"

When it came time to settle the tab, I gasped, "Oh Boy! That's a doozy! Well, since I put the last tab on my room and the ole boy has gone to bed," I thought, "I'll put this tab on his room. After all, he was here for part of it." Needless to say the next morning as I entered the lobby, I saw my co-worker pacing frantically at checkout. He was animated, yelling at the clerk, and looking back and forth at me.

I was still half in the bag and just hoping to hold it together long enough to get on my flight back to NY. He came stomping over to me, holds out the bar tab with his name, room number, and my scribbled version of HIS signature, and asks, "What in the hell is this?" I don't know exactly what I said, but I do know I confessed half-heartedly by trying to explain I didn't want both nights on my room, so I split them up. To say it went over like a fart in church would be the understatement of the century.

Imagine a seven-hour flight from San Francisco to LaGuardia sitting next to a guy who wants to rip your throat out. If I wasn't still hammered from the night before, I might have even felt uncomfortable. A few

Bloody Mary's and a seat change fixed any lingering remorse.

When I arrived at work on Monday, I didn't even make it to my desk before I was called to the CFO's office. It had been two days, but I hadn't sobered up. I told the truth again. The truth got me fired, as it should have. My boss cried, and I wanted to; but I just gathered my things and left.

Let's look at the decision point in my story. Had I taken option 1, I might have watched him in the lobby, conjured up the appropriate lie and drug it to the bitter end. I also could have told him the truth, and then calculated that a lie to my boss would make the new guy look like the liar. Deep down, I would know I was a liar and totally wrong.

Under the second option, the acutely in-tune person would have realized the lie was telling himself he could pull off the lie in the first place. That person knew even drinking in the bar with an expense account was bad news. If he was really honest with himself, perhaps he knew, even prior to going to San Francisco, things would be bad.

You see, we know ourselves better than we like to admit. Instead, we search for the outcome that feels good, the one that will fulfill our most basic instinct: the pleasure principle.

Now that was a lot of talk to get us to one singular point. Are you ready to get honest? If you truly want things to change, you'll have to start with yourself.

"Most can see other people's faults. A few can see other people's virtues. And two or three can even see their own shortcomings."
- Ancient Sanskrit Verse

LESS THAN

Ever ask yourself questions like, "Why am I so different?"

You and I are no different from the rest of the world. Everyone will instinctively try to put their best foot forward. They are going to conceal their emotions and try to appear confident and calm. It's just like the saying goes, "Never let 'em see you sweat!"

As Americans, we spend hours upon hours, and millions of dollars, trying to dress ourselves up. We care about appearance. And for what? Do we hope people will think more of us than we think of ourselves? We become stuck thinking we are different than everyone else: not as smart, not as good looking, not as bright, not as articulate, not as popular, or not as self assured.

Well, there's something you need to know and memorize: <u>you can't judge your insides by other people's outsides</u>. We are all the same inside. We all ask the same questions, have

the same insecurities, and struggle with the same deficiencies. What we have is a spiritual malady. We have a disease that causes us to see the world through a set of colored lenses; our perception is skewed against us.

I've had enough compliments to last a lifetime about how smart, funny, motivated, and talented I am. When I hear this, the first thing that enters my head is: "If they only knew who I really was." Guess what? They do know who I am, and you know who you are. We are as smart, funny, talented, and gifted as everyone says we are. We are unable to see it, but it's true. The sooner we start believing it, the better our lives will become.

You might have been the most popular person at your school, but somewhere deep down inside, you felt different. You felt alone. All those friends and all those masks added up. It created a backlog of lies and self-perceptions that would eventually become insurmountable. I'm almost certain it's what drove me to drink the way I do. It's so hard for us to disclose our deficiencies. Why is that?

Nick Vujicic, a motivational speaker with no arms or legs, obviously cannot hide his disability. He has chosen to find ways to do the impossible. Not only does he live a quality life, he has impacted millions, encouraging them to give their all in life. If he can do what he's done with his handicaps, I'm thinking you and I don't have anything to complain about and absolutely no limitations. And if we give our all, the world might be astounded.

We are more than conquerors and we will win this war raging inside of us the same way Nick did. He gave it his all one day at a time. Oh, we definitely have a few hurdles in front of us, but I'm all in. How about you?

"Everyone has inside of him a piece of good news. The good news is that you don't know how great you can be! How much you can love! What you can accomplish! And what your potential is!"
- Anne Frank (1929 -1945)

WHAT A DIFFERENCE A DAY MAKES

There are certain moments in your alone time when you sit and reflect on how much you've hurt the ones you love. It doesn't really matter if you're sober or not; although, it's much worse when you are sober. You think about the enormity and depth of the harm you've caused, or may still be causing. Although the people you are concerned about probably wouldn't believe you if you told them, and for good cause, your feelings are genuine.

Your thoughts create an energy within you; it's a displaced energy in raw form. It's a ticking time bomb of indecision. You're not sure if you want to start the reconstructive path of fixing your beleaguered past or completely avoid the whole thing and slip off into your oasis of inebriation. I can tell you I've chosen the latter over the former on too many occasions.

An alcoholic's emotions are a lot like water; they take the path of least resistance. And, unfortunately, that path is almost invariably the path of inebriation. It's the easy way out; it's the one that requires no accountability, no sacrifice, and no effort. It's also the one we've battle tested over and over again: the familiar.

Sometimes it feels like your world is closing in on you; it's a suffocating chamber of misery and loneliness. God seems to have abandoned you; you question whether or not He ever loved you. Hope becomes a four-letter word, and is usually accompanied by other four letter words. You debate whether going on, or letting go completely, is the best path. You want to scream, cry, or maybe whirl off into a fit of a rage. Nothing is clear and nothing feels right anymore. You've left the city and burned down the bridge behind you. You've become an island of self-pity and self-loathing has become your dwelling place.

As you ponder your circumstances, a heat rises up within you, and you feel consumed and defeated by life and the cruel hand it's dealt you. Somewhere deep inside, you know it's entirely your fault, but that only makes matters worse. Now you feel broken and worthless. How can this ever be fixed? Is it even worth fixing?

Even your most loyal supporters have given up on you. "What on earth is there left to live for," you ask. You feel the end is drawing near and you welcome it, like a long lost friend you haven't seen for years. A final resting place, where there is no struggle, no more hurt, no more disappointment, and no more loss. Your musings of it as a means to an end in your thoughts become frighteningly serious.

I don't have all the answers to feeling like this, but I wouldn't be writing this today if I didn't at least know one thing. You MUST not believe the lie that your life is  ending or over. Dinah Washington won a Grammy in 1959 for a song called, *What a Difference a Day Makes;* it was later covered by such greats as Tony Bennett and Frank Sinatra. Look it up on the Internet and give it a listen. No truer words have ever been spoken. Give yourself some time to weather your emotional storm.

It's amazing what a difference a day will make if you can hold on. Even when the apocalypse of addiction is upon you, and the worst of your emotions have besieged on your every thought, it will pass; sunnier skies lay ahead. I can't tell you how to opt out of the shame game, but I can tell you it *will* end. Like everything in life, whether good or bad, it can't last forever.

Go for a walk or take a ride with a close friend. Keep moving, and eventually it will go away. The clouds will lift and the four-letter word of hope will soon be accompanied by better four letter words like love, help and home.

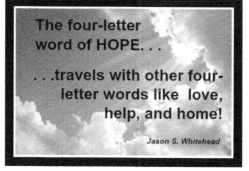

The four-letter word of HOPE...

...travels with other four-letter words like love, help, and home!

Jason S. Whitehead

It may be that you are all you have left, so the answers must come from you and your Higher Power. If you pray and ask for forgiveness, things will change. I can't promise tomorrow will be great, but I can assure you it will be better.

"Happiness is like a butterfly which, when pursued, is always beyond our grasp, but if you sit down quietly, may alight upon you."
- Nathaniel Hawthorne (1804 – 1864)

TEMPTATION ALLEY

As you undertake this thirty day journey, there are going to be times your addiction fuse is so short almost anything will be sufficient reason to go back to the well one more time. It's going to call you on a physical, mental, and emotional level. You will have little to no defense against it. It's why we sometimes refer to our entry into recovery as "the gift of desperation." Desperation might be the only reason why you avoid the temptation.

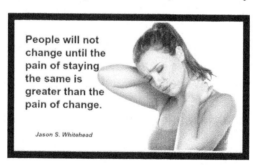

People will not change until the pain of staying the same becomes greater than the pain of change.

What happens to the alcoholic in his first thirty days is as predictable as unpredictable. They are going to be restless, irritable, and a virtual fountain of emotional turmoil. On a conscious level, they are dealing with memories and emotions they have dulled out of consciousness for days, months, or even years.

Friends and caregivers must be ready to practice a patience and empathy they most likely have never been called upon to exhibit. It is key they understand these first thirty days are a painful period and subconsciously hard on the alcoholic. The alcoholic is stirring his or her emotional cauldron and searching for a reason to leave. He is looking for any excuse to return to the call of the alcohol.

If friends and family are not able to extend a surplus of forgiveness and overlook outbursts, they may inadvertently be playing right into your addictive thinking. Thoughts like, "I knew they wouldn't understand," "I'm sober now, and things are still miserable," and "If they try to confine me or come at me one more time, I'm just going to go get drunk. It's easier that way," begin to swarm the frontal cortex. Given any excuse to flee recovery, we most certainly will. Wisdom dictates that you, your friends and family avoid emotional entanglements for at least the first thirty days. It will serve you both well. It is summed up best in the Big Book of Alcoholics Anonymous, "One careless, inconsiderate remark has been known to raise the very devil. We alcoholics are sensitive people. It takes some of us a long time to outgrow that serious handicap"[2].

---

[2] Bill Wilson, *Alcoholics Anonymous*, The Family Afterward (Alcoholics Anonymous World Services, Inc. 1939) 125.

In short, stirring up the skeletons of yesterday's closet will booby-trap your recovery before it even begins.

There's a popular saying in the recovery community that states, "If you don't tell on your disease, your disease will tell on you." The idea is that when you feel like you want to drink or use, you need to tell someone. Publicity is a great defender against our illness. The problem I run into is my ego. I want to feel like I'm in control and I don't need anyone's help to beat this thing. After all, I got myself into this mess; I can get myself out.

The problem is that this is a lie. It's true the primary onus of recovery is square on your shoulders, but it doesn't have to be entirely on you. There are people in our lives who want nothing more than for us to be and remain sober. Call on them. Read this chapter with them.

Talk about your feelings and theirs. They will be anxious to learn and understand more about you. They will be better informed about how to help, how to understand your outbursts, and better armed to help you make it through the day.

Everyone wants to be a part of your feel-good story, even strangers. Look no further than AA for the epitome of this idea at work. When you are feeling tempted, the first policy is being honest with yourself. When you can do that, you can take action. Then take the second step and tell someone about it, perhaps even a stranger. Vocalizing your temptations is like letting air out of a balloon. The pressure to use will slowly dissipate.

You'll build your skill at deflecting temptation and gain confidence that you truly can be in control.

Before you know it, you will be equipped to handle things the next time you are walking down Temptation Alley.

"Complete abstinence is easier than perfect moderation"
- St. Augustine of Hippo (354 – 430)

PARADISE LOST

I remember the very first time I decided to quit drinking FOREVER. Just the word *forever* seemed to echo off into infinity as if it were some impossible, unachievable unit of time I was doomed to endure. What does "I can never drink again" mean? What about things like marriage, childbirth, retirement, or catastrophic events? There will never be another reason good enough to drink again? My head hurt just thinking about it. I was mad at myself. How could I have abused a privilege so much I could never use it again? It was true; all my fun tickets were gone. The alcohol carnival was closed for good.

After I managed to allow the anger and bewilderment to roll away, a deep depression began to settle in like a black cloud poised to lay siege on the foundation of the rest of my life. I began to course through all the possible reasons why drinking might be acceptable just once more: a major death in the family, a winning lottery ticket, or news the world was going to end. It was a cruel game of fantasy, and I was the only one playing. Eventually, I saw the foolishness of it all and quit harping on forever-land. The cloud, however, did not go away.

Do you remember Pig Pen from *Peanuts*? He always had a cloud of dirt and dust following him. This forever-type sobriety was my albatross, my curse, and my cloud of dirt and dust. I was unhappy and lacked any real joy. I had entered a grieving process. I was grieving the loss of my dearest, and perhaps only, friend of so many years. King alcohol had been with me through the good times and the bad, through college and a failed relationship, promotions, and job losses.

It was always there. It picked me up when I was down and turned the mundane into the intriguing. The aggregate banality of recovery was suffocating. I certainly couldn't live with alcohol, but I didn't know how to live or have fun without it either. There was no more joy. It was my very own Paradise Lost.

Learning to live all over again was not easy. It took time and effort. I had to step out of my comfort zone and leave the security of that rough, distant exterior I use to keep everyone in my life at arm's length. It meant talking to strangers, opening up to people, and being transparent, especially when it hurt to do so. It meant being responsible and accountable, showing up when I said I would, and being reliable. I had to get outside myself and begin helping others when I'd become a master of selfishly focusing on my own needs and wants.

Recovery is a new journey. It's about enjoying the simple things in life and taking risks (not the drinking a liter of vodka and driving around kind of risk, but emotional and relational risks). It requires trusting people and engaging in life, doing things you always wanted to do but had always manufactured some meaningless reason why you couldn't.

There is FUN in recovery. Get out there and grab life by the horns. Go on that tour of the city, visit a museum, climb that mountain, take a trip to the place you always wanted to go, see a show, enjoy the county fair, try a new restaurant, etc. Quit making excuses for yourself. Live a little. You haven't lived in years and its time you make

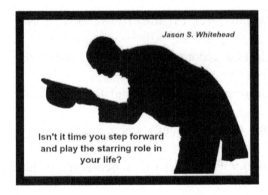

up for it. Get out there and take on the world. Isn't it time

you step forward and play the starring role in your own

life? Your future awaits!

"The greatest discovery of my generation is that a human being can change his life by changing his attitude of mind"
- William James (1842 -1910)

RAINY DAYS

Did you wake up to a rainy day today? Score! Why shouldn't it rain? You even like the fact it is a rainy day. You don't want people outside, and you definitely don't want people running around happy. You're miserable and want others to be miserable, too. Let's call it a generous gesture on your part: spreading the wealth.

I remember one rainy morning back in 2007. I had just lost my job (again). I was fired as manager of a TGI Friday's restaurant. I got so drunk the night before I could hardly close the store. An ex-kitchen manager took over the duties as best he could legally; but, the alarm was never set. We had a visit from our regional manager the very next day. My fate was doomed.

My fiancé was amazing and understanding as always, even though there was no excuse for what had happened. The next morning, as I lay in bed, she faithfully woke up, got ready, and left for work in the rain. I remember taking a large pull off the bottle of vodka lying underneath my bed. As I looked out the window watching her walk down the sidewalk, her hair swung like a pendulum of sorrow and disappointment. It was more than I could bear. I was devastated. My heart broke in places doctors can't even see.

Here I was, 33 years old, unemployed, lying in bed, and totally worthless. I had to watch a beautiful young girl, who hated her job, trudge that lonesome journey to work so we could stay afloat. I bawled like a baby that morning, and then proceeded to get more inebriated than I had been in a long time. By the time she returned home that evening, I wasn't even a shell of the man she had agreed to marry. I still get a little choked up when I think about that particular rainy day.

1 Corinthians 10:13 says, "No temptation has overtaken you except what is common to mankind. And God is faithful; he will not let you be tempted beyond what you can bear. But when you are tempted, he will also provide a way out so you can endure it." I had my way out from under it; however, I chose to keep drinking even though I knew better. It was no one's fault but my own. I tried for years, but to no avail, to drink that fact away.

What are you going to choose? Do you really want to continue to stack up rainy days filled with regret over lost jobs and broken relationships? Are you going to deny what you know to be the truth? Are you going to keep yourself stuck in a self-imposed rut?

Try toughing it out this time. Just once, give it a real go at least just for today. Who knows, maybe the clouds will clear, the sun will shine, and you'll be the one

setting off to make your mark on the world.

"Reject your sense of injury and the injury itself
dissapears"
Marcus Aurelius (121 – 180)

THE PEOPLE UNDER THE STAIRS

If you're going to be spending most of your free time in church basements, and there is a good chance you will, then there are a few things from my own experiences that may illuminate your path.

How could I ever forget the first meeting I attended? I was living in a small town with my parents after losing yet another promising career in New York. I had returned home for the summer in defeat. Someone suggested I attend an AA meeting.

As I walked into the meeting room, I became abruptly aware I was the only one there under 60 years of age. Apparently, I was the only non-smoker to boot; I don't even think I was a coffee drinker at the time. It felt like I was in the sequel to Wes Craven's horror film entitled, *The People under the Stairs*. They looked like zombies to me. They were fixated on my presence, as if I were the first fresh meat they'd seen in months. Perhaps I was the first newcomer in months. I soon noticed there was something very strange about these zombies; they were all smiling and seemed a bit jovial.

I scurried immediately to a chair as far away from the group as possible. I tried not to look directly into anyone's eyes for fear I may turn to stone or, even worse, have to speak. It was a futile effort. One of the zombies came rumbling toward me, introduced himself, and handed me a laminated piece of literature to read aloud. I was officially trapped. The people under the stairs had me in their clutches.

After suffering through the first few readings, it was my turn to read, and it felt like the spotlight was on me. I read something called *The Promises*; what a bunch of hooey those were. I might as well have read the *Lucky*

Charms commercial out loud. Seemed like pink hearts, yellow moons, orange stars, and green clovers were more likely to come flying straight out of my behind than for all those promises to come true. Either way, I played along and was relieved when it was all over.

Now I could sit back and blend into the scenery like I had intended from the very beginning. Wouldn't you know, they had the audacity to announce that, due to MY being there, this would be a "1st step meeting." They announced this as if I was some drunken guest of honor. I was mortified, but my attitude would soon change.

As the meeting agenda unfolded, the zombies went around the room and told their unyielding stories of the mayhem and debauchery that had landed them in this basement. There was a whole lot of laughter, and there were even a few tears. One by one, they regaled us with their seemingly refined versions of personal life destruction. There were tales of horrific arrests and broken marriages, lost jobs, and estranged loved ones. Hot dang! They were just like me, or maybe I was like them. It didn't really matter. I just knew at that moment, I was a zombie, too.

I still didn't like the idea of being one of them, and tried my best not to show it for fear they might try to initiate me. But deep down, I knew I was in the right place. I was stuck in Wes Craven's nightmare: my nightmare, my life. My name is Jason W. and I AM an alcoholic.

Like Paul on the Damascus Road, the scales had fallen from my eyes; extreme denial, however, is hard to break. Despite the revelation of truth, I left that day in a state of terminal uniqueness. I was like them, but they weren't like me. This type of thinking would be the first of many mistakes I've made in my recovery process. The

truth is we only need one thing in common: our illness. The rest is inconsequential.

So get to an AA meeting today, take your seat and listen. Even when it doesn't make sense, just listen. For once in your life, take someone's advice other than your own. It might just save your life.

"All truth passes through three stages. First it is ridiculed. Second, it is violently opposed. Third, it is accepted as being self-evident."
- Arthur Schopenhauer (1788 -1860)

RISK, REWARD, AND REALITY

"So I'm feeling better physically, although I tire easily. I want to do everything and nothing all at the same time. I'm so mixed up I can't stand it. Do I want to run or do I want to walk? Do I want to stay awake all night or sleep all day? Do I want to have sex or never have a relationship again? Do I want to eat everything I can get my hands on or just starve myself to death? Do I want to quit talking to everyone forever or run out into the streets screaming? Am I content with the future of my life or ready to commit suicide? I can't feel anything and yet I seem to feel EVERYTHING. I'm a walking paradox. Don't talk to me please, but God forbid you ignore me, I'll kill you—literally. Not literally, of course, but it sounds right in my head when I say it that way."

I'm pretty sure this is what a captive animal feels like right after capture. It's grieving for its freedom and ready to cut you to ribbons if cornered. Leave it alone, and it will leave you alone. Leave it alone too long, and it will get away. As alcoholics we are really like that, you know. We just want to be left alone; but if you leave us alone too long, we are going to escape. Unfortunately, you know exactly where we're headed when we get out.

Boy, what a bad idea; and yet, it's the one we just can't shake. It's like a moth that is drawn to the flame. We know we are going to get burned. WE KNOW IT. And yet, we fly right into it, blinded by its false beauty and deceptive glimmer. Between my feelings of being two feet tall and my twisted reasoning, I surmise that getting burned is worth it. Why not be a moth.

I know you are thinking, "So what is it about all of this doom and gloom? Isn't there supposed to be hope? You said there would be hope and I just needed to believe. I mean, I do hope I can get a drink soon, and I absolutely believe I can make that happen just given a little more time." Isn't that what we think? Well, it's what I think anyway; unfortunately it's what the majority of us are thinking in the first couple of weeks. We rationalize, "I could quit for a couple days, but a good night's sleep, a few good meals, and God forbid a paycheck, and I'm off to the races and will see you on the other side of misery." Let's be clear, the euphoria always turns to agony.

Of course, I can't ever remember that truth when I need it to come to mind. If I've had one good night of drinking in the last ten years where I had fun and suffered no consequences, but I'd had a thousand nights of no recollection, embarrassing moments, wrecked vehicles, lost relationships, disappointed loved ones, and pissed away money, I will remember that one good night while I'm standing in the liquor store line. It's practically instinctual. It's beyond our control.

It's physically and literally tied into the reward center of our mid-brain known as the amygdala. It tells us we had a good time once and we can have it again given the right input to our blood stream. The amygdala has no conscience, no arrest warrants, nobody to disappoint, and no consequences. It gets a cocktail for the Fourth of July and it whistles *Dixie*. All it knows is it wants to whistle *Dixie* again. The rest is irrelevant to the amygdala. I'm not giving you license to use, but you need to be informed who your opponent really is. You need to be aware just how far inside your camp it has dug in and now lives.

There's more to recovery than good and bad days.

So how are you doing right now? Are you in your first two weeks? Are you a year sober, or maybe multiple years? Is there a blue chip on your nightstand or in your wallet? Do you have a medallion on display?

Do you even know what I'm talking about? If you've been where I've been, then it doesn't matter. You know exactly what you need to know. You've got an uphill battle against the likes of something you have never faced before.

No matter how good or bad you feel today, you need to be armed. You need to be prepared, because the enemy is not just something that's trying to kill you, the enemy IS YOU!

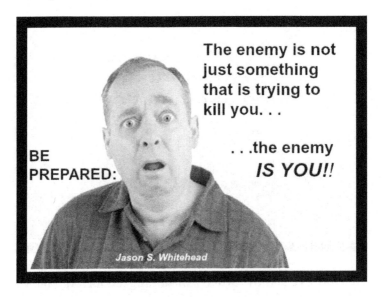

What's your battle plan for today? Trust me, your enemy has a plan to destroy you today. You are the general of your army. Be vigilant, be prepared, be armed, and be on guard. The only thing between you and victory is your ability to choose what's right

when the battle is upon you.

Suit up & show up!

"And God said "Love Your Enemy," and I obeyed him
and loved myself."
- Kahlil Gibran (1883-1931)

SELF-IMAGE

You're probably wondering by now if your self-esteem and self-worth will ever get any better. In spite of yourself, you probably still traipse around town as if no one can touch you. Hey, maybe no one can. You know somewhere deep down inside, however, that you are lower than low. You feel inadequate and useless. You are keenly aware you are a disgrace to the ones who love you the most. At least you feel this way inside.

You're awkward in social situations and often overcompensate, especially when drinking at times no one else is.

1)   You become rude and stand offish. At least no one can get close to you, assuming that any of them even want to try.

2)   You veil yourself as aloof because it provides a shelter of superiority. If you can just come off as better than someone, then of course, you must be. Depending on your victim, they just may buy into it. It's all smoke and mirrors; but, it usually works.

3)   You decide to take the quiet and distant approach, a skill I've honed and perfected since childhood. I stay out of the way, observe, and, like a chameleon, I blend. I can isolate right in front of you; you won't even see it happening. I'm a master; your social skills are no match for my uncomfortable silence. Test me; I dare you!

So what do we do about all this? How do we regain our lost esteem and worth? Do we start going to mixers and recovery events and miraculously transform into social butterflies? Can we jump on a bus to nowhere and start over?

The way to regain self-esteem is by doing esteem-able acts with gratitude and humility (two concepts we all but left for dead years ago).

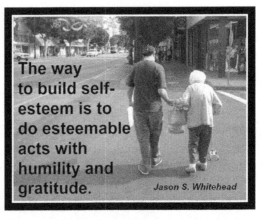

We can choose to let our light shine or we can shine in and of ourselves.

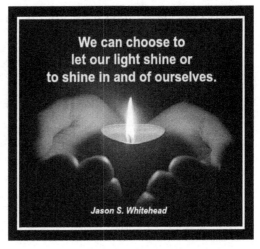

The way to keep your self-esteem is to be authentic: REAL! Be the same person you look at in the

mirror while brushing your teeth, no matter where you are or whom you're with. Don't try to impress. Just be you; you are amazing. Throw away the masks and relate to others. Listen to them. Care about their struggles. Be transparent. The people in our lives don't love us because we are perfect; they love us because they can relate to us. So quit the games and just be present with them in the moment.

Just for today, try to have a few genuine conversations with those in your life. Seek first to understand them without asking anything in return. You'll walk away feeling great, and so will they. You will both be looking forward to your next chance to get together. That's what it's like to build instead of tear down a relationship.

You can sign up right here and now. The day is waiting to embrace you. Your family and friends are waiting for the real you to show up. Today might be a good day to surprise them.

"It is not the strongest of the species that survives, nor the most intelligent. It is the one that is most adaptable to change."
- Charles Darwin (1809 – 1985)

WHAT ARE THEY THINKING?

Ever found a hole-in-the-wall deli or a swanky little café somewhere down a back alley; it's almost impossible to find, but you managed to stumble upon it. It looks intriguing and the menu in the window sounds absolutely delectable. You're not sure what it's like, but it's worth a try. Right? For whatever reason, you decide to go in. You sit down and order the house special. Maybe you order an old standby you practically challenge them to impress you with, because you've had it a million times somewhere else.

You and your dinner companion engage in really meaningful conversation, and the atmosphere just fits the mood like a glove. The food arrives and you look at each other; your culinary prospecting venture has struck edible gold. It has presentation, flavor, and has truly met your taste buds with a palatable bliss. The dining experience is delectable, and the conversation flows as well as it began. You both agree you will be back time and again, and you can't wait to tell others of your find. A few years pass and the place delivers every time, just like it did that very first time.

One day, however, you return and the meal is not like you remember. Have they changed some of the ingredients? Did the cook have a bad day? You wonder if they've changed ownership. You shake it off as a bad day and know you'll be back again. The months go by and you keep returning to your old dining treasure, as you draw upon the memories of how great it was the day you found it. You occasionally change menu items hoping to find the one thing that's still amazing. Coming up short each time, you still feel the food is a worthy cause, and you'd hate to write the whole place completely off just because it's no longer the best kept secret in town. This is what it's like for the alcoholic.

There is something that seems so comfortable about sitting at a bar, staring at a wall of liquor bottles, and listening to the tunes blaring through the speakers. It's like nothing exists in the whole world except what's directly in front of you. The bartender is catering to your every whim, people are jovial, and discussions are opening up between strangers everywhere. All of the problems you've been facing disappear and one of your favorite tunes may even breeze across the stereo waves at just the right time. I'm at home in that moment and I don't want to leave. I'm not alone anymore. There are people just like me to my left and to my right. I fit in. Not only do I fit in, I'm at the top of the food chain. The place of security I've searched for since my childhood is in my grasp. It's "a bird in the hand," as the adage goes.

It will only last as long as the alcohol does, but that's far from my mind at the time. Numbness has replaced pain; I am happy. I am the master of my own destiny; my future is limited only by my imagination and the longevity of my buzz. I may meet my future spouse or conceive the next million-dollar idea. The night is unpredictable, but it's good; I know I'll be back.

You see, we may have hundreds of horrible experiences to recount from our days of drinking, but we only remember the good ones. We just keep going back, holding out hope the next time will be like the first time, or at least maybe it will be better than the last. As a dog returns to its own vomit, so does a fool to his folly.

So the next time you ask yourself, "What was I thinking," the answer is pretty simple. Just as Eve sought after more in the Garden of Eden, so does the alcoholic. Always searching for more. It doesn't make it right or normal, and it definitely doesn't make for a good excuse. But, at the very least I hope I've pulled back the curtain so you can see the why we are unable to see the truth behind our malady.

You and I understand the reasoning. But, it's time to find a new favorite locale; the old one should be condemned and shut down. Continuing to do the same thing hoping for different results is indeed the definition of insanity. We've been caught in the centrifugal force of our actions based on false paradigms. Time to eject from our own private nightmare.

Eventually, we must face the futility and carnage of our reasoning. What are we going to do about it? What might create that sense of belonging, peace, and joy that does not include alcohol? Can we replace those memories with memories of real relationships and real joy? The answer my friend is a resounding, YES!

"We have a hunger of the mind which asks for knowledge of all around us, and the more we gain, the more is our desire; the more we see, the more we are capable of seeing"
- Maria Mitchell (1818 – 1889)

THE ANGRY FACE OF FRIENDSHIP

People who care about us often get angry at us, especially after a relapse. It's not that they are mad at us particularly for the person we are, but they are frustrated that we can't get it right. They want us to get sober so badly, that when we fail, they get angry. It's the same reaction you experience when your favorite team loses a close game. You love the team and want so badly to see them come out victorious; when they come up short however, you get upset. You aren't usually angry with the players themselves; you are more frustrated at the situation than you are at the actual team. You know they've played the game well, but something went wrong. Mistakes were made.

We all need someplace, somewhere, or someone to pin our frustrations on, so it usually comes out on the people we love. It was a helpful revelation when I was able to discern the anger being pointed at me was over the relapse and desire for success and not directly at me as a failure. They were mad at the scenario. It's much easier to cope with the complex emotions of anger if you can connect with why they are there. We want so badly for those around us to understand us that we take scarce little time to understand them.

It would be a great injustice if we did not make an effort to do <u>for</u> them what we so desperately ask <u>of</u> them. The people in my life tell me it's like living with two different people: the one they love, and the other who is trying to kill the one they love. So when the intoxicated version of me stands before them, they see the one they hate.

So take a deep breath. Know the anger needs to be vented and dissipated, most likely at the intoxicated you: the version of you they hate. Despite all evidence to the contrary, they still love the authentic version of you.

Don't take offense and hold a grudge. Just let them get it all out. Anger and frustration need to vent. It's making them sick; let them get it out.

If they really love you, they will still be there for you. Reason will soon return and you can both get about the vital business of recovery . . . for just one more day anyway.

"We forgive principally for our own sake, so that we may cease to bear the burden of rancor"
-Buddha (c.563 – c.483)

MECHANICAL FAILURE

It was an otherwise normal and uneventful night back in 1985 when I was only about ten years old. I was staying at my friend Alex's home for the weekend. We were playing, as kids do, with any and everything we could get our hands on. I remember sitting on the floor of his bedroom. When I looked up, Alex appeared from the darkness of the hallway with something I only vaguely recognized in his hand. It was a brown, hourglass-shaped bottle with a white label that read, "Michelob Light."

I wasn't particularly excited or adrenalized as much as I was confused. I thought to myself, "What are we supposed to do with this?" With a mischievous grin, he asked if I wanted to try beer. I didn't really want any, to be honest with you, but my parents had slipped me sips of Strawberry Daiquiri's and Pina Coladas before. They didn't harm me, so why not. After all, I didn't want to be a wuss.

We sat in the evening shadows of his bedroom that night and split the Michelob Light. I don't recall feeling much of anything after drinking it. I definitely cannot associate any feelings of euphoria or otherwise good vibration coming from our indulgence. Quite frankly, I mostly felt guilty and unimpressed. It would be another four years before I drank again.

Flash forward to my teen years. I was living like a fish out of water in Key West, Florida after the abrupt passing of my mother. I was desperately trying to recreate the tight knit social confines of a former prep school kid who is now a small fish in a big pond and of a cultural minority. I was struggling. How was I supposed to penetrate the local social scene? I wasn't a local, otherwise known as a *Conch*. I had no Cuban roots and only had known two black kids in my whole life.

Alas! An invitation to a keg party from a kid who lived just a few blocks away. When I arrived a few nights later, I walked into what seemed like a snake pit of social awkwardness. Everyone but me knew everyone. Everyone seemed to be drinking so naturally and comfortably. I poured a cup of the golden elixir from the tap. I was a social butterfly by the time I saw the bottom of my second cup. I don't remember much else about that night, except that I had been accepted; I was now *in* with the locals. All the barricades of my insecurities had melted away with each beer; it was the answer to my prayers. I now knew how to defeat my social anxieties and climb the social ladder.

This became the false conclusion that has haunted me for the rest of my days. Rather than build solid, honestly come by coping mechanisms, I would forever be imprisoned by the lure of the liquid solution.

It's important to look at our lives and discover what voids we are filling with our addictions. Mine was introversion and social anxiety. Take some time for self-reflection and introspection; discover what you might be hiding or trying to overcome. We have to get honest with at least ourselves so we can leave behind a past filled with deceit and false assumptions.

Today is the day to face the world without assistance from a deceptive substance. Don't run and hide from your insecurities. Just for today, rely on just you, your networks, and your higher power. You can do this.

"The cruelest lies are often told in silence."
- Robert Louis Stevenson (1850 – 1894)

MAYBE WE TOOK THIS TOO FAR

It's easy to look back on your life and slip into a melancholic state as we reflect on how we have conducted ourselves over the years. Our minds can quickly fill with big screen images of all the disappointments and embarrassments we have endured from our substance abuse. We were probably very inebriated for most of them; yet, they are just as vivid in our minds as the flashing images on the billboards of Times Square. Firmly fixed in our subconscious are images of days we were treacherously hung over at work or social gatherings. We were barely hanging on by a mere thread, as we struggled desperately to conceal it until we could get to the next fix. We hold painful memories of the times we didn't show up when people counted on us to be there. We even hoard memories of moments we were physically present but can scarcely remember a thing that happened.

Spend just a few minutes walking down this memory lane, and the pile of baggage we're dragging with us is destined to gain momentum and roll right over us from behind, crushing us underneath the weight of our own remorse and guilt. Around the next corner we run head into questions that can never be answered: "What if I had done that differently or what if that just had never happened?" They course through our brains like a surging tide, as we desperately search for an answer or reason why we ended up in this pit of shame and despair.

These thoughts become infectious and debilitating, creeping into every corner of our consciousness, quickly souring the fruits of our recovery. *Maybe we took this too far.* Maybe this recovery is only a prelude to our next failure. We tell ourselves no one believes we are going to make it anyway. No doubt everyone is holding their breath until we fail again. They are simply hiding behind empty words of encouragement, yet are poised to say, "I told you he wouldn't make it." No doubt your mind is saying, "Maybe they're right. Maybe I *am* a failure. It's what I've secretly felt all along anyway."

STOP right there!

If you find yourself lost in a whirlpool of self-loathing and doubt, you must correct your thoughts immediately. The specter of self-condemnation makes quick work of its victims and will swiftly dispatch all the hope you have.

Maybe you did take it too far. Who are you kidding? Of course you did.

Second-guessing is not an activity exclusive to alcoholics and addicts. Everyone walking around planet earth is second-guessing some event or course of action they took or some critical decision that changed their

lives forever. I want you to understand there is a certain togetherness we share with one another through our imperfections. There is a bond of suffering between all humankind that allows us to understand what it's like to hurt, regret, and wonder how things could've been different.

My story is of alcoholism; yours may be of homelessness, growing up without parents, a business failure, lost love, or missed opportunity. There are people who have lost everything to great catastrophes or natural disasters, and still others who are forced to live with terminal illnesses that are not of their doing. They are all second-guessing their lives in the same way we are. We are not alone, although it feels that way more often than we care to admit. Maybe we took this too far.

Maybe it could have been different. Maybe our destiny took a wrong turn.

Rest assured you can never change the past by thinking about it; you can only change the present by going about it.

It's over, done. That story has ended. Turn the page. Drag yourself back into the present moment and go about living in today; then going forward to tomorrow, when you think about yesterday, there won't be anything to regret.

Maybe we get it right this time. Maybe we just get it right today. It's a good place to start.

"There is no sense in punishing your future for the mistakes of your past. Forgive yourself, grow from it, and then let it go."
- Melanie Koulouris

THE CHRONIC RELAPSER

Simply put, relapse is part of recovery. Not everyone experiences it, but many people do and many times over. Let me tell you something about having multiple relapses. It can be one of the most miserable recoveries you can have, especially if you manage to achieve a decent amount of clean time leading up to your relapses. You thought you felt like a failure before you got sober; now you have not only failed in your attempt at life, you have also failed in your attempt to recover. You may become an outcast from the recovery community because you are seen as a bull shitter; you are labeled as someone who isn't doing their step work or who can't get honest with themselves.

While it's true I have seen people fail for those reasons, I have also seen many fail who gave it their all.

Some of the most knowledgeable people in recovery I know have had two or more relapses. They are people who have helped countless others, people of influence, people with all the gifts to heal and teach, yet they are laughed out of recovery circles for the inability to get it right. Nothing they say will ever hold weight again, at least for two or three years, despite how accurate, profound, and useful there information may be.

Much the same attitude is given us by those outside of recovery, but for entirely different reasons. Where people once thought we were capable, bright, and promising; they now only see weakness, risk, and failure. We can't get jobs with people who know us. We are straining to conceal our plight for fear we will be outcast from society all together. Our families have disowned us, and our friends have given up and moved on with their lives. Even the people who believed in us the most begin to doubt their judgment. We are left to fight this battle alone.

Only the strongest people in recovery and in our lives stand with us. If we are to survive, we must draw from their faithfulness and move forward in their love. We do not stand alone. There are millions just like us: people who have failed and gone forward and people with 20+ years of sobriety who are tricked to revel in the futility of those first few attempts.

You are not alone and you are not starting all over again. You have simply taken a knee; you need to get back up and dust yourself off. If a baseball player gets three hits out of ten trips to the plate, then he bats .300 for the season and is an All-Star. So if you're like me, and have a few successes followed by a few failures, just remember you can still be an All-Star. You simply need to get back to the plate and start swinging that bat.

Once you swing, you might shake the stigma of relapsing and become *the chronic recoverer*. Your friends will now likely come from sober circles instead of recovering ones, but your goal is recovery and not friendship. Keep that close to the vest. Press on—just for today.

"Life is not about how many times you fall down. It's about how many times you get back up." - Jaime Alfonso Escalante (1930 – 2010)

A ROOM WITHOUT WALLS

Since starting on the path to recovery, there have been some restrictions placed on me: different ones at different times, for many different reasons, and by many different people, including myself.

Let me start by saying that in the first thirty days, you might as well slap me right in the face and spit in my eye if you levy restrictions against me. I can't see the logic in them. I don't want anything in my life to change; I simply want the consequences to stop. They hide my car keys, seize my bankcards, keep me from my friends and loved ones, flush my sedatives down the toilet, and may make me go to meetings. They've even gone so far as to take my cell phone—my lifeline. Why the nerve! These things are all I have left of my manhood, my independence, and my freedom. They are all I've got and they want to take them from me? Get them out of my face!!!

I want to scream, "You don't know what I need! I'll get it all back together. Just watch me. I've dug myself out of worse than this. You all just need to leave me alone. Who are you to take these privileges from me anyway? I'm a grown adult. I screwed all this up myself and I will fix it myself. What do you think these rules are going to do; help me? Ah Shit! Of course that's what you think. What's worse is that I know it, too; but, I don't want to give up. I don't want to give in. I've still got a dog in this fight. You're trying to tell me I can't even manage my own belongings and that's just absurd. Isn't it? I mean it cuts right to the bone and I'm already fragile. I just need time and space. I need a room without walls! Somebody get me outta here!"

Any of that sound familiar? The *Big Book of Alcoholics Anonymous* would call this "self-will run riot," a complete and utter denial that anything other than our own wishes are what are right for us. To an alcoholic, restrictions feel like a potentially lethal injection. The truth is these things are administered as if a lifesaving surgery is about to occur.

It feels like giving in to someone else's direction will kill you, and we'd rather take our chances alone than give into the recovery process. Of course the odds are a lot better on the recovery path, but we don't see it that way. It's the same immoveable perspective that brought us to our knees to begin with. The idea that somehow we know what's best and that we'll get it all figured out *our* way seems to be the only realistic solution.

If there are ever any groundbreaking discoveries into the world of addiction, I am certain our ability to surrender is where the most impact will be made. Until someone is willing to do almost anything to get well, their chances are limited. As for those pesky guidelines; you don't have to like them; you don't have to agree with them; you don't even need to see the value in any of it at all. What you do need to do is deal with it. Like the Nike slogan says, "Just do it!"

The irony of the recovery process is that the more you do to restrict yourself, and the more safeguards you have in place, the more freedom you actually have. Take for example someone with an allergy to peanuts. They must constantly be aware of what foods they are consuming. But if you told them they could only go to restaurants where nuts were not served, they would be free to eat anything on the menu. For those of us in long-term recovery, sobriety is our room without walls, and limitations are our guideposts. You don't have to do anything you don't want to do, but as Ashton Kutcher said in a speech to America's youth at the 2013 Teen Choice Awards, "Opportunity looks a lot like work."

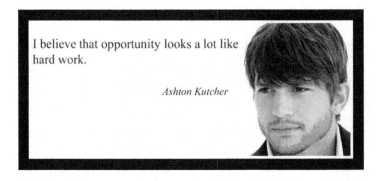

I believe that opportunity looks a lot like hard work.

Ashton Kutcher

I'm here to tell you that recovery is work and to be successful, you just may have to give up some stuff along the way.

So don't focus on all the things you are losing, instead focus on what you are gaining: the opportunity to be free from addiction. If you don't, the next thing you lose could very well be your life.

"To get completely away from our aversion to the idea of being humble, to gain a vision of humility as the avenue to true freedom of the human spirit, to be willing to work for humility as something to be desired for itself, takes most of us a long, long time."

- Bill Wilson (Alcoholics Anonymous)

ALONE WITH A MONSTER

I was driving down the road in my car going virtually nowhere. I'd set out with just a thought it would be a nice day for a ride; there wasn't much else to do on my day off. Besides, I didn't want to sit around the house and let my samurai mind cut my accomplishments to shreds with the notion life had become mundane and futile again.

Maybe I'd frequent one of my favorite local retailers or go by the vegetable stand and peruse their fresh goods for the evening's dinner. It was pretty normal stuff really. Suddenly the wheels in my head started turning. Like a master thief casing his next hit, I began to break down the situation at home. How could I make today a drinking day? First, I had to get all the appropriate times of departure and arrival straight. Then

I needed to formulate a good reason to be distant and avoidant. What was feasible? What made sense? What could I say and do to keep the others at arm's length without raising any red flags?

It's really a lot like chess. Each move becomes calculated and is cognizant of subsequent moves. How would the dominoes fall in my favor? How would I sneak my bounty into my lair? It wasn't long before I realized I wasn't alone anymore. I was alone with a monster: a monster that wanted me dead. It was the kind of monster that will tell me everything's going to be ok in the presence of a self-induced shit storm.

This kind of monster says, "There's nothing wrong with

just one drink," even though we all know one is too many and a thousand is never enough.

And just like that, I was in the middle of a liquor store. All the details worked out to surgical precision; I was indeed a virtuoso of my deceitful craft. The problem is the only thing I was crafting was my own demise. I'd created a self–built doomsday machine I would marvel at only long enough to take a drink and wind up at odds with the world yet again. At the time though, it seemed so worth it, so simple, so secure, and even deserved. You probably know exactly what I'm talking about.

It takes a long time to get to where you can trust yourself completely. I'm not sure I've ever reached that point, but I do know there are things you can do to help your cause. It takes a long time for the physical cravings to leave even when you are unaware of their direct presence. Like a stalking butler, they are in the shadows, lying dormant until the right time to strike.

We are not a weak-willed lot, you know. It took a whole lot of will power and persistence to get into this mess in the beginning. It has nothing to do with weakness. In fact, you are likely the strongest-willed person you know. The problem is when you think you are by yourself, you are actually alone with a monster. That monster is inside you. It consists of your memories, low self-esteem, guilt, shame, and your ever-persistent desire to feel different.

The monster desires to feel empowered, at ease, confident, and comfortable; he seeks to be without worry, concern, or doubt. It's the monster that lives inside all of us. Our monster has a drug of choice; it knows what it wants to consume, and we know how to feed it. People without chemical dependencies sometimes feed their monster with food, work, exercise, cigarettes, caffeine, television, pornography, and much more. The luxury they have that we don't is that most of their monsters will not kill or completely destroy them, at least not in short order. It may take them slowly, or not at all.

We've got a much bigger battle to fight; a potentially losing battle. Even those who manage to live a whole life in addiction only succeed in a Pyrrhic victory.

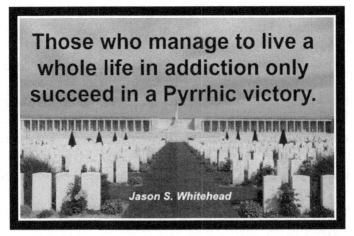

Their conquest of life in addiction does not outweigh the cost of the battle.

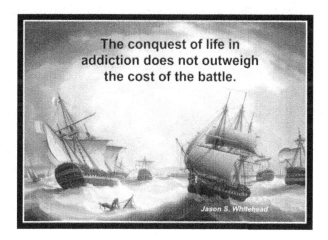

We need not fantasize we can or will endure this kind of punishment.

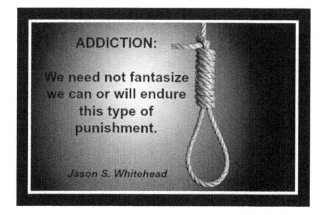

There is nothing gained from a life lived incapacitated, without awareness, and alone.

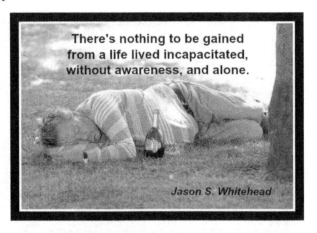

So how do we win our fight against an enemy we cannot see, this enemy inside? There is an old Cherokee adage that contains our answer. The elder chief is teaching his grandson about life. "A fight is going on inside me," he said to the boy. "It is a terrible fight and it is between two wolves. One is evil; he is anger, envy, sorrow, regret, greed, arrogance, self-pity, guilt, resentment, inferiority, lies, false pride, superiority, and ego." He continued, "The other is good; he is joy, peace, love, hope, serenity, humility, kindness, benevolence, empathy, generosity, truth, compassion, and faith. The same fight is going on inside you - and inside every other person, too."

The grandson thought about it for a minute and then asked his grandfather, "Which wolf will win?" The old Cherokee simply replied, "The one you feed."

Which one are you feeding?

"Do you not believe that there is in man a deep so profound as to be hidden even to him in whom it is?"
- St. Augustine of Hippo (354 – 430)

WILL YOU BE THERE?

I'll bet many of you have severely damaged, and perhaps even destroyed, the relationship with the one person in your life whom you love the most. They might be the only person who stayed in your corner through it all. They've been there long after they should have been, that's for sure. It hurts, doesn't it?

Just a glimpse of clarity and all of the sudden you have that *holy shit* moment when you recognize what you had/have. And now, it's all hanging by a thread. The entirety of that sacred relationship hangs in the balance of your recovery.

Hold on; all might not be lost. Let me get real gut level with you, though. Thirty days and a cloud of dust aren't going to cut it. You've tried numerous times to convince them you are through, only to go back like a dog returning to its vomit.

We go out and destroy ourselves, then come home, and try to make a half-baked apology. Because we are good at convincing even ourselves, we can also convince others that things will be different. Almost Pavlovian-like, they believe us and salivate at the prospect of our getting well. After all, when we're sober, we're pretty swell people.

So if thirty days, and more love and support than we deserve, aren't enough, what is? The problem is up to this point you've been putting Band-Aids on a deep, bleeding wound. Believe it or not, one of those Band-Aids is our drinking. Drinking isn't the origin of our problems; it is merely a symptom manifesting from a very deep wound. We are a three-part being: body, soul and spirit. One part of our basic being, if not all three, has been severely damaged. Most all recovery curriculums target the spiritual side. Effective curriculums target all three components of our being. Face it; things are way out of balance and Band-Aids aren't enough. We have to tunnel through to the root cause of our wounds in all three areas:

Body: Our physical relationship to the rest of the world is more important than we often give it credit. Have you suffered an injury or dealt with something as simple as high blood pressure (hypertension)? Are you a recluse or socially avoidant? Most alcoholics drink to feel different. That could be to avoid physical pain or the discomfort we feel around others. Are there root physical issues you need to address? Start with an inventory of your social interactions to evaluate if they are healthy. Perhaps you need to get a physical from a medical doctor. Once any issues have been addressed, you can tackle your problems with knowledge and understanding.

Spirit This is our connection with our higher power. Most of us as addicts don't want someone to play the God card on us. We know we need a connection with our higher power, but avoid it at all costs. We've called out for help in our darkness over and over, and we are still in a mess. So don't tell us we need God. Where is He when we need Him? Besides, we are sure He, like everyone else, is fed up with us and has turned His back on us anyway. The real problem is that we have created our own God: alcohol. We run to it with all our problems and have created our most intimate relationship with a bottle.

What you need, however, is a deep and meaningful relationship with your Higher Power. He wants to be your friend: the one you walk and talk with and lean upon. He's waiting for you to want and love Him more than anything or anyone. He wants you to turn to and find all you need in Him, not a bottle. It's the first commandment: love the Lord your God with all of your heart, soul, and spirit. Get this one right and you'll be able to handle life's challenges, because you'll no longer be doing so alone.

Soul: This is the seat of our emotions and feelings (encompasses our mind, will, and emotions). Most addicts are not good at handling either. Our drug of choice has become the perfect prescription for drowning out our overwhelming feelings of discomfort. We want the hurt to stop. What is the deep wound you are trying to mask? Do you suffer from anxiety, depression, PTSD, or been diagnosed as bi-polar, etc. Medication can help with body chemical issues that cause some of these illnesses.

If this is part of your recovery story, let me warn you: finding the right medication is a daunting task and not for the faint of heart. You may be the lucky one they prescribe the perfect medication, in the exact right dosage, the very first try. Most likely that will not be the case. Finding the right issue to address, and honing in on the right medication at the perfect dosage level for you, is a trial and error process. These trials can pile on top of previous failed attempts. You will need an advocate to watch over you, observe the way the drugs are affecting you, make sure you don't miss a dose, and watch for side effects. It is not wise to do this one alone.

Find a counselor and get all of the things that cause you to suffer out on the table. Find new ways of viewing situations so you can cope with feelings of regret, remorse, anxiety, and fear.

If you want to be there for your loved ones, and have them there for you, you have to tackle the root causes of your problems. This may come in the form of time-out so you can wrestle with these cornerstones of life. The rest of the world might call it rehab or recovery. It's simply time for you to right your body, soul, and spirit. Don't fight it. Embrace it. If not, you'll fall apart over and over.

It's time for you to decide. Look deep and be honest with yourself. Do you need help? Will you keep struggling and failing, or will you reach out for help and come home ready to be there for your family and friends?

"Nothing can stop the man with the right mental attitude from achieving his goal; nothing on earth can help the man with the wrong mental attitude."
-Thomas Jefferson (1743 – 1826)

DOWN WITH THE SHIP

There are so many dynamics to recovery I could spend the rest of my life studying, practicing, honing, and transforming while never reaching a definitive end. In fact, most anyone you meet in recovery is going to tell you to do exactly that. There is one principle, however, that is paramount to your success; there is only one that has a definite beginning and finite end. To put it simply: we have to give up.

If you're still not too keen about the God thing, the process of giving up by itself will get you several steps closer on its own merit. When I give in to the fact I am not the master of the universe and cannot will anything into existence, let alone my own sobriety (and oh how many times I've tried), I soon discover things begin to go quite well. On the other hand, when I roll that white flag back down the pole to even half-mast, in an effort to only partially surrender, things begin to turn out quite poorly instead.

The thing you must understand about this surrender process is you are really only surrendering to yourself and your own selfish ways. You don't have to lose face or concede to some other person. You simply need to quit butting heads with the man in the mirror.

When I was growing up, I knew I wanted to be a professional football player. Even if God had given me the athletic ability, my size and speed were issues I could never conquer. My body was limiting in this way. In the same way, my mind and body have limited my ability to drink successfully in moderation. There are just so many things in life I want to do, but cannot. To admit I can't conquer this one substance seems unbearable. Why? Do I owe it to somebody? Will I be seen as a failure? Am I less of a man because of this? The truth is the only one in the whole world who even cares that I can't conquer alcohol is me. Practically everyone else in the world wants me to quit; they even admire my decision.

The bottom line is we are not on some giant vessel at sea, tossed about by the throws of alcoholism, destined for the eye of the storm. The only thing sinking here is our reputation and the respect of those we love. We are sailing for a victory over dependency and the only way to do that is to veer away from our alcoholic storm.

So step to the captain's table of life and raise the white flag high. Surrender to the clear skies ahead. There is no honor in going down with THIS ship.

"The greatness of a man's power is the measure of his surrender"
- William Booth (1829 – 1912)

LIFE WITHOUT A CRUTCH

There are so many times in life when we are disappointed: a lost job, an imperfect date, a loved one lets us down, our favorite team loses, or perhaps we just didn't get what we wanted. These were drinking occasions for me. I always served alcohol at my pity parties.

Someone once told me addiction is "repeating successful measures;" and it's true. No matter what the disappointment, drinking successfully helped me cope every time. It was the most reliable thing in my life. I never finished a fifth of liquor and felt the same way I did before I started. It was so successful I drank no matter what I felt. I didn't even need catastrophes anymore. A busted shoelace, a rainy day, dinner was burned, I didn't catch any fish; it didn't really matter. Drinking became the answer to everything or nothing at all.

Before I knew it, I didn't even need a reason to drink; I simply drank not to feel anything at all. Any real coping mechanism I had cultivated became some relic stowed away in the memory banks of yesterday. The only steam I knew how to blow off anymore smelled of 80 proof vodka. And just like that, I had untrained myself completely on how to deal with life.

It quickly became evident that getting sober was so much more than throwing out the bottles and canceling my daily trip to the liquor store; that was the easy part. Now I had to figure out how to go about this whole life thing. I was left emotionally naked and any recollection of normalcy was lost somewhere in the sea of booze that had recently washed me out. I had no instruction manual and there was no thirty-day refresher course offered in town. I quickly realized life without a crutch was difficult and dangerous work.

To say re-entry into the world of sobriety was something I wasn't prepared for is laughable at best. People pissed me off, work stressed me out, and traffic was always a nightmare; every little thing that didn't go my way sent me into a tirade of emotional

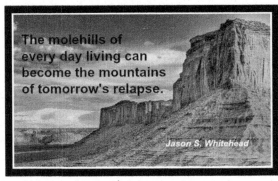

meltdown. I became short with the people I loved, lost patience with life, and found no reward in any small victory I was able to conjure up. Suddenly, the molehills of everyday living had become the mountains of tomorrow's relapse.

I couldn't find happiness in anything. I blamed it on things like debt, my job, or a relationship. I think I even once blamed my dog for pooping on the carpet. Happiness was a myth and any I sought was completely conditional. If I only had *this*, then I would happy. If you would just stop doing *that*, I would be happy. If this one thing were just *different*, I would be happy. What I was really saying is, "if I could just down a liter of bourbon right now, I would  really be happy." It's important we stop this type of thinking. We must begin to find happiness in the small things and stop focusing on all of the things we cannot change.

Conditional contentment is a moving target. When life begins to creep up on you again, and you are feeling squeezed in from all sides, remember your old successful measures are not available to you anymore. Having patience for the people in your life, including yourself, is a far greater tool than alcohol ever was.

You're not dealing with anything the rest of the world isn't facing. It's imperative you pop the bubble of terminal uniqueness incubating your addiction and face what comes at you like everyone else. After all, you know you should have been doing this all along.

Soon, each little victory will become another weapon in your arsenal of coping skills for the future. Life without a crutch will get easier and easier. Then, before you know it, you will see it feels good to walk again!

"If you aren't in over your head, how do you know how tall you are?"
- T.S. Eliot (1888- 1965)

CATCH ME IF YOU CAN

How does it feel when you are hiding things?

You know exactly what I'm talking about. It's the times you are hammered, but everyone else assumes you're sober, at least for a little while anyway. You're trying so hard to act normal, you inherently act weird. You overcompensate in your false reality, hoping you come off sane. You might get away with it once or twice, while those around you walk away wondering, "What's gotten into him?" But deep inside you know your charade is over, your mask is slipping. Suddenly, you realize you may be worse than ever, and the only person you've been fooling is you.

If you are around family or close friends who really know you, there is no hiding. Your unwitting tells signal them you may be intoxicated. I've tried to figure out what my tells are so I can minimize them. Apparently, however, they are things I cannot control: the way my muscles hold up my eyelids, the cadence of my words, the volume of my speech, or my reaction times.

While we try to hide from friends, family, and coworkers, we also feel the need to hide from complete strangers. Fresh clothes and some mouthwash ought to do the trick. Maybe just a pleasant smile and a quick-witted remark will conceal my identity. I'm not sure how many retail clerks I've tipped off in my time but I'm sure it's far more than I care to admit.

Just like children, we alcoholics learn the ABC's of excessive drinking very quickly. _A_lways _B_e _C_hanging your hiding spots or points of purchase. I'm sure I'm not the only one who knows ten routes to the same destination to avoid certain areas or a particular intersection where local officers might see me. How many times have we created an excuse to go to the store or visit a friend when all the time, we know we have an ulterior motive in mind. Ever visit different locations so the store employees won't snipe out your issues? To play off Jeff Foxworthy; "if you know where every liquor store is within twenty miles of your home, you might be an alcoholic."

So, how does it feel to hide, all the while knowing you are fully exposed? You don't need to answer that question; I already know the answer and it isn't pretty. Isn't it high time we quit walking in the shadows?

So what if you decide to step out of the darkness and quit hiding? This may be a physical task, a mental one, or both. Just stop running. It's a good idea no matter where you are in the recovery process. Simply drop the veil. We need the people who love us to know what we are facing. Tell them the demon inside is on the prowl today, driving you to find and consume.

If they don't know, their desire to help or protect you will be virtually impossible and you will become combatants. Recovery cannot hit a moving target. By unveiling the plans the demon inside is asking us to pursue, we disarm him while strengthening the relationships with those who care for us.

No more hiding. No more running. Our greatest weapon against this disease is full disclosure. Darkness must flee in the light. So sit down with your support group and get honest. Tell on the enemy inside. Then, together, map out a plan for the day that will strengthen your resolve and keep you safe just for today.

"Man is not what he thinks he is, he is what he hides."
-André Malraux (1901 – 1976)

CRAVINGS

You're craving a motivational buzz; you know the one I'm talking about. I don't care if you're gulping shots, sniffing glue, or shooting heroin. You want the buzz that makes you say, "I can tackle the world; I feel good today." You need a boost to keep going that, once induced, says, "Yeah, everything's going to be ok."

How did we get here anyway? How in the world did we become dependent on an outside substance to dictate what our day will look like? Does it really matter? Not anymore. And it shouldn't matter to you either, because you're here now. You can't change the past; you can, however, influence the future by taking appropriate actions in the present. Let's just deal with the reality of it all and move on from here.

In my first thirty days, my cravings focused on a bottle: a bottle of anything with 40% or higher in it. You might be craving the same, or perhaps you're craving something else, but you want something to make today run smoothly. You need something to take away the jitters, reduce the edge, or go up your nose long enough to have you walking on sunshine. Eventually, the physical cravings will leave, but it's that mental craving that is the true specter in our daily battle.

I went out for some errands one morning. I didn't go far and my purpose and intentions were clear. Still, my car wanted to proceed to a place I didn't need to be. The cravings had not gone away; they may have even gotten worse. It will take more than this book, or any other like it, to relieve you of these demons. They *will* go away though. For some it will be the next day, for others it will be six months, or a year from now.

Do not be discouraged if everyone else in recovery acts as though everything is fine. It's not!

Sometimes it's easier to act our way into right thinking than it is to think our way into right acting.

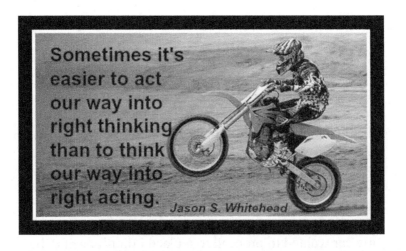

Simply try to do the next right thing one day at a time. You may even find yourself doing that very thing in no time at all. Recovery is not a thinking man's game, it's a doing man's game.

Look at each craving like an instinctual lie. It's an inborn defect in our physical makeup. Our reward center is after something that will numb us in the short term and kill us in the long run. My personal nemesis even kills its creator. In order for alcohol to be produced,

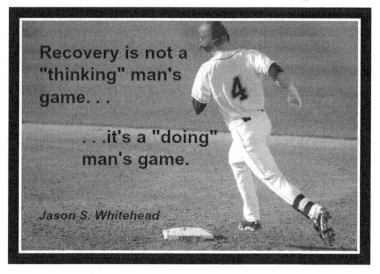

it requires yeast, but when the alcohol content reaches about 14%, the yeast is killed and only alcohol remains. The very thing we think we need to survive is the pathway to death.

As children we clung to myths and legends for a sense of peace and security. Unlike those legends that were put in place to bring about joy and wonderment, our self-made myths about substances are only causing pain and destruction. Realize them for what they are, and stand strong. A craving is nothing more than an inward denial of an outward solution.

Set your mind on the future and walk it out day by day; we cannot grow beyond our last unhealed wound.

Do not allow a craving to pick at the scabs of recovery before they have a chance to heal. Instead, be diligent and stay busy with the activities of sobriety.

I personally find I do best when I take a few minutes before bedtime to take a gratitude inventory

followed by time to establish my activity plan for filling the next day with positive and productive activities. Good planning and action are your allies and your antidotes.

As Mother Teresa said, "An idle mind is the devil's playground." Find positive things to fill your mind today: quotes, meditation, a good book, a service project: whatever can fill the space formerly held by a craving—just for today.

"As soon as you trust yourself, you will know how to live"
- Wolfgang Von Goethe (1749 – 1832)

THE DEVIL INSIDE

We've all had our fair share of experience with self-examination. After all, isn't that how we sit around and torment ourselves on a daily basis? We take an unfavorable moment in time and roll it back over and over in our heads. It's like one of those devastating hits you see in a football game: the camera crew shows the play again and again from every angle, to see just how bad it really was and which image makes it look the worst. Isn't that what we do with our arguments, our confrontations, our failures, or perhaps even an arrest? What could I have said or done differently? Why did I allow them to do that? Who do they think they are? If only this had never happened? We've destroyed our lives over these moments, thoughts, and ideas. It's almost like there's a devil inside and he controls what we watch on our mental television. The further along we get in our addiction, the more channels he controls.

It gets to a point where it's not just self-reflection anymore. Soon we can't control our emotions, words, or actions as they are unfolding. Words come out all muddled and wrong; we are angry and depressed. We may have been completely sober for days and we're still saying things we don't even mean.

After some of these episodes, I was able to recognize I was talking, or sometimes screaming, in my alter ego's voice. Mr. Hyde became nearly impossible to stop even when I knew he was directing my paths. He'd been allowed too much control. I'm not suggesting we are schizophrenic or psychopathic, although addiction does take people to sanitariums and often death. I have not been sentenced to either one, nor do I ever plan to be. What I am suggesting is that this nefarious projectionist, the one who was controlling my thoughts, need not be fed his drug of choice, or any drug for that matter.

So how do we stop the tapes from playing? Better yet, is there a video store that sells a new release? The solution for this one will require you take action. You first have to immediately put a stopgap in play *every* time the tapes start to play. Just STOP! Get up, take a walk, sing a song, cite a favorite verse, or quote that saying you've hung on the wall—whatever; just don't let those old tapes start to spin.

But don't stop there. You must begin to write truth on your tapes. My friend created a list of all the good qualities she saw in me; she framed it and placed it on my desk where it sits to this day. When my old tapes begin to play, I pick it up, start reading it (out loud if necessary), and remember this is the man I truly am.

I've started writing down the good things people say about me or quotes that inspire me (some of which are in this book). So buy a journal or use the last page in this book to begin your list. When the devil inside wants to condemn you, just flip to the back of the book; it will remind you that you are indeed a winner.

Don't let your past write your story in your mind or in your life. It's history. You can't undo it, but you don't have to dwell there. It's ok to just move on. Today is a beautiful canvas waiting for you to 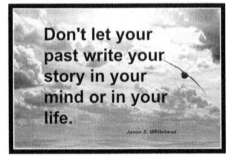 write a new chapter. Tomorrow it will be added to the pages of your past, changing the course of your story and its future. It's how we make a new tape.

"We fall back into the past, we jump ahead into the future, and in this we lose our entire lives."
- Thich Nhat Hanh (1926 – Present)

HAVE I ARRIVED?

I've heard time and time again that if we don't learn from history, it is doomed to repeat itself. It's very much like the scientific method of trial and error. We take experimental steps to solve a particular problem; after the first effort fails, we move on to another method, continuing the process until we get the right combination of factors without repeating the failures of our earlier efforts. There's one caveat: if the problem begins to evolve and change, then so must our solutions.

After my first year of sobriety (the first time), I remember thinking, "I've finally got it licked!" What was all the fuss about anyway? I am the master and commander of my wants and desires. I will never drink again. I looked at those who were falling like flies back into the pit of despair and labeled them as weak. I knew they weren't serious about their recovery; they were reaping what they put into the recovery process. Even when I wasn't saying it, I was thinking it. How ignoble, how rude, and how pompous I was. Who was I to call them *weak*? I was barely out of the fog myself. In short order (about another year to the day), I had fallen just like them: so quickly, so abruptly, and so damn deservedly. I had become exactly what I had so sternly judged others to be just a few months before.

Not only that, I stumbled at least a half dozen times more before I regained my footing. I had lost the winning formula; where did it go? What happened to being the master and commander? Who was the finger pointed at now? I was a complete mess and I knew it. I had all the tools and all the knowledge anyone could ask for, and I couldn't get sixty days to save my life.

There is a saying in recovery that goes, "You can't save your face and your ass at the same time."

How apropos. I was so busy trying to act like I knew what I was doing, I forgot to do the things that got me my first year and 11 months to begin with. I was no longer the juggernaut of recovery I once fancied myself. History had, in fact, repeated itself over and over again.

You can never forget where you came from, or you will indeed find yourself back there again. It's about humility, compassion, empathy, selflessness, and especially surrender.

I've had my share of trials and more than my share of errors. I know now what I did not know then: recovery is not a destination; it's a journey. Much like life, there are only new challenges and new hurdles. There is only one stopping point, and I'm not in a hurry to get there. You will never arrive in this journey; you will only change directions. Buckle your seatbelt and enjoy the ride. But, always remember where you came from, else you wind up back there again.

"There is nothing noble in being superior to your fellow man; true nobility is being superior to your former self."
- Ernest Hemingway (1899 – 1961)

BE SOMEBODY!

Now that I've been blackballed by society, past employers, and most of my loved ones, where do I go from here? How do I get back on my feet? Where am I going to find a job? I've had so many good jobs and several shots at a real career, all of which I have flushed down the drain. Everyone thinks I'm just going to screw it all up again, so why bother?

Part of me thinks they are right; how can I convince them they are wrong? Better yet, how can I convince myself they are wrong? At times I just want to escape to one of those Alaskan Snow Crab fishing boats where I will either perish or become some hardnosed fisherman who has $30K in his pocket two or three times a year. I'd fit right in: just me, the Bering Sea, and a few lowlifes who are probably just a couple bottles of bourbon away from being right where I am.

Realistically, I know that's not an option. I've got to fight it out here on my home turf.

Even if I go into treatment, the inevitable job search still looms on the horizon. I can't hide those misdemeanors. They'll know right away what I am. Am I good enough to forge yet another career? I've burnt so many bridges.

Let me ask you a question. Were or are you good at your job? Are you one of the best to ever undertake your trade? When sober and present, weren't you one of the best men for the job? Weren't you the go-to guy, the guy everyone relied on? And just think, you did all of that while you were hung over, intoxicated, or dreaming of being intoxicated. You were a real hot mess, and you were still one of the best in the game.

Now just imagine if you could do all that while you were riding the white horse, chasing dragons, or getting into the cups on a daily basis, what you might be able to do sober. You were only a shell of what you could be, and you were still one of the best.

What do you think you might be able to do now that you are sober?

Maybe you're still detoxing, and just getting to and from the bathroom is a task; your capacity is limited.

But as you heal, you will get bored, and eventually will feel motivated. You will get back out there and you will be amazing. You will be amazing because you already are amazing. You've always been amazing, but you allowed a substance to mask your abilities.

You've been hiding from everyone, even yourself. Well, it's time to clear the slate; "Tabula Rasa." Get out there and fulfill your destiny. Be Somebody! Somebody amazing! Be the amazing YOU!

"When you have confidence, you can have a lot of fun.
And when you have fun, you can do amazing things.
- Joe Nammath (1943 – Present)

BABY STEPS

The sunlight streams through the window as you pull the covers back over your head and say, "So here I am getting started again." It's like picking up the beer cans and emptying the ashtrays the night after a big party. You're hung over and miserable. All you want to do is clean up the mess and get rid of the stench so you can lie down and relax in a cool, dark place. You desperately hope you can put behind the vague recollections of the mayhem you brought to those around you the night before. As memory rolls over you like a crashing wave, you cling to a hope against hope that no one dare bring up the many methods by which you embarrassed yourself.

Recovery is the same way. The only difference is it's more than just one party or one weekend. It could be a lifetime of wreckage you must own up to and face down. I know you're longing for a cool dark place to hide and heal, but this time it's going to be a little different. There will be sunlight and accountability. There will be relationships and debts to be paid. There will be emotions and new coping mechanisms to try. It's all very scary I assure you. I've been terrified of the future. You can't even trust yourself, not yet anyway. But in time, even that will come.

You can't microwave recovery. There are no shortcuts.

It's just you and Father Time trudging along and working it out day by day.

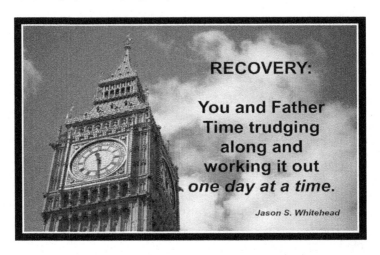

Hopefully, deep down inside you have a sense this recovery thing is in fact possible. Even though there are still many parts about yourself and your life you would change, you cling to the thread there is hope.

Yes, I know that sometimes all that anger and frustration still washes over you. You are petrified one wrong move will land you back on your ass again. So before you begin those first baby steps into a life of recovery, here's my meager advice born from painful experience:

1) Don't rush headlong into your finances or you will become easily discouraged. You didn't spend it all in one week and you won't fix it all in a week.

2) Don't try to win back the hearts of those you hurt. Allow them their time and space to heal. They will come back to you in *their* time, not yours.

3) Most importantly, just relax a little and stay in the moment.

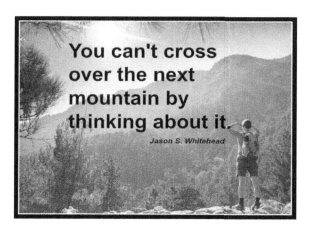

You can't cross over the next mountain by thinking about it.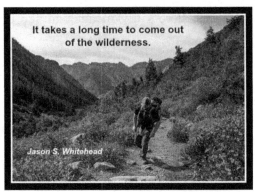
It takes a long time to come out of the wilderness.

As the wise saying goes, "Life is a marathon, not a sprint." We will all be waiting for you when you get here. So for today, take baby steps: rest your body and mind, believe in your future, and commit to the change you have made these past thirty days. You can do this—one day at a time.

> "All of life is a journey which paths we take, what we look back on, and what we look forward to is up to us. We determine our destination, what kind of road we will take to get there, and how happy we are when we get there."
> - Anonymous

EPILOGUE

Unfortunately, I know from personal experience this first thirty days has been the longest month of your life. Hopefully, by now you are feeling better physically and emotionally. I pray you have found spiritual connections and renewed relationships. But this is just the beginning of a journey you will need to map out and navigate for the rest of your life. No one will do it for you. It will involve adding disciplines to your daily routines: nightly gratitude inventories, meditation, learning to be transparent and authentic, exercising, and possibly medications to keep your body and mind fit for the challenges ahead.

It's important you find ways to keep your head about you when all around you feels shaky. There's a saying that goes something like this, "The good thing about getting sober is you get your emotions back; the bad news is you get your emotions back." We are good at using alcohol to drown our emotions; now we must find new ways of resolving conflicts and dealing with hurt feelings, loneliness, frustration, etc. Take a class, get some help on line, see a counselor: whatever it takes. It won't be easy to learn new coping skills, but you can do this!

Antoine de Saint Exupery said, "A rock-pile ceases to be a rock-pile the instant a single man contemplates it, bearing within him the image of a cathedral." So you've piled up a few rocks in your life; what might you make of them?

You've made it through the roughest patch; you'll make it the rest of the journey just as you did these first thirty days: one day at a time.

I'll leave you with my daily conclusion to my morning meditations:

"Today looks like

a great day

to have

a great day!"

Jason can be reached at jaswhitehead@gmail.com
This book may be found online at Amazon.com

Made in the USA
Monee, IL
09 March 2020